Through The Eyes Of A Child

Six Worship Services And Dialogues For Advent Through Epiphany

Gail Gaymer Martin

CSS Publishing Company, Inc., Lima, Ohio

THROUGH THE EYES OF A CHILD

Copyright © 1999 by
CSS Publishing Company, Inc.
Lima, Ohio

The original purchaser may photocopy material in this publication for use as it was intended (i.e. worship material for worship use; educational material for classroom use; dramatic material for staging or production). No additional permission is required from the publisher for such copying by the original purchaser only. Inquiries should be addressed to: Permissions, CSS Publishing Company, Inc., P.O. Box 4503, Lima, Ohio 45802-4503.

Scripture quotations are from the *New Revised Standard Version of the Bible*, copyright 1989 by the Division of Christian Education of the National Council of the Churches of Christ in the USA. Used by permission.

Library of Congress Cataloging-in-Publication Data

Martin, Gail Gaymer, 1937-
   Through the eyes of a child: six worship services and dialogues for Advent through Epiphany / Gail Martin.
      p. cm.
   ISBN 0-7880-1519-2 (pbk. : alk. paper)
   1. Advent. 2. Christmas. 3. Epiphany. 4. Worship programs. 5. Children's liturgies.
I. Title.
BV40.M38   1999
263'.91—dc21   99-37637
                                                                                                                CIP

ISBN 0-7880-1519-2   PRINTED IN U.S.A.

With much love to my husband Bob, who supports and encourages my writing ministry. Also to my goddaughters Kathleen Buetenmiller, Jamie Pineau, and Natalie Wright, who, as adults, continue to love Jesus and lead lives strong in their faith.

Table Of Contents

Preface	7
Introduction	9
Advent I Advent Past, Present, And Future	11
Advent II Jesus Came To Earth	19
Advent III Jesus Will Come Again	29
Advent IV Lord Jesus, Quickly Come	39
Christmas Christmas Through The Eyes Of A Child	49
Epiphany Epiphany Through The Eyes Of A Child	61

Preface

So often during worship I have listened to a children's sermon and enjoyed the simple, clear message of God's Word. The illustrations and examples provoke uncomplicated yet accurate answers to a child's questions about church history, traditions, and biblical truths.

With this thought in mind, I designed a series of six worship services from Advent through Epiphany in the form of dialogues between an adult and a child. Studying the events from a child's perspective provides opportunities to explore biblical history and traditions, to explain prophetic truths and events of Christ's birth, and to acknowledge God's remarkable plan for our salvation. These worship services are a learning experience for both children and adults.

Introduction

This book contains six worship services from Advent through Epiphany. The format for each is similar and includes a dialogue between an adult (pastor, youth leader, or parent) and a youth. Each service provides a bulletin format and dialogue script. The format allows flexibility for traditions of individual congregations, such as the inclusion of the Eucharist or the service of lights. When a service of lights is used, small individual candles with drippers should be distributed to worshipers as they enter the sanctuary. Music used throughout the services may be sung by choir, congregation, or both, as presented in the bulletin format. The music selections in the format are suggestions only. However, hymns and anthems, selected in cooperation with the Minister of Music, should reflect the basic themes of each service.

The four services of Advent share a common opening sentence from Psalm 24. Also two verses of the hymn, "Come, Thou Long-Expected Jesus," serve as a congregational reply to the responsory reading for each service. All six services share the common reading from 1 John 3:1-3 which reminds us that we are all children of God and wait for the day when we will know God personally and understand all things through his eyes. Bible verses are from the *New Revised Standard Version*.

The first four services define the meaning of Advent and then explore the traditions and elements of Advent, preparing for Christ's coming in three ways: Past — his birth, Present — his example for living, and Future — his coming again in judgment. The Christmas dialogue returns to the words of the prophets and explores the concepts of darkness and light, sin and salvation. Epiphany celebrates the Good News to the Gentiles, but most important, Jesus' presence in our lives today. The final service concludes with the thought that discipleship is not easy, but we are commanded, as part of the community of believers, to spread the Good News of salvation to the whole world and to baptize. We are left with the challenge to follow in the footsteps of Paul and Barnabas, continuing their work in the world today.

Worship Bulletin

Through The Eyes Of A Child

Advent I

Opening Statement: Psalm 24:7-10
Pastor: Lift up your heads, O gates! and be lifted up, O ancient doors! that the King of glory may come in.
All: **Who is the King of glory? The Lord, strong and mighty, the Lord, mighty in battle.**
Pastor: Lift up your heads, O gates! and be lifted up, O ancient doors! that the King of glory may come in.
All: **Who is this King of glory? The Lord of hosts, he is the King of glory.**

Opening Hymn:

Advent Responsory: Psalm 89:1- 5, 8 and 85:8-13
Pastor: I will sing of your steadfast love, O Lord, forever; with my mouth I will proclaim your faithfulness to all generations. I declare that your steadfast love is established forever; your faithfulness is as firm as the heavens. You said, "I have made a covenant with my chosen one, I have sworn to my servant David: 'I will establish your descendants forever, and build your throne for all generations.' " Let the heavens praise your wonders, O Lord, your faithfulness in the assembly of the holy ones. O Lord God of hosts, who is as mighty as you, O Lord? Your faithfulness surrounds you.

All sing: "Come, Thou Long-Expected Jesus"   Traditional Tune
**Come, thou long-expected Jesus,
Born to set thy people free;
From our fears and sins release us;**

> **Let us find our rest in thee.**
> **Israel's strength and consolation,**
> **Hope of all the earth thou art,**
> **Dear desire of every nation,**
> **Joy of every longing heart.**

Pastor: Let me hear what God the Lord will speak, for he will speak peace to his people, to his faithful, to those who turn to him in their hearts. Surely his salvation is at hand for those who fear him, that his glory may dwell in our land. Steadfast love and faithfulness will meet; righteousness and peace will kiss each other. Faithfulness will spring up from the ground, and righteousness will look down from the sky. The Lord will give what is good, and our land will yield its increase. Righteousness will go before him, and will make a path for his steps.

All sing: "Come, Thou Long-Expected Jesus" Traditional Tune
> **Born thy people to deliver,**
> **Born a child, and yet a king;**
> **Born to reign in us forever,**
> **Now thy gracious kingdom bring.**
> **By thine own eternal Spirit**
> **Rule in all our hearts alone;**
> **By thine all-sufficient merit**
> **Raise us to thy glorious throne.**

Preparation And Prayer: (1 John 3:1-3)
Pastor: See what love the Father has given us, that we should be called children of God; and that is what we are. The reason the world does not know us is that it did not know him. Beloved, we are God's children now; what we will be has not yet been revealed. What we do know is this: when he is revealed, we will be like him, for we will see him as he is. And all who have this hope in him purify themselves, just as he is pure.

Let Us Pray: Heavenly Father, we come to you with the joy and innocence of a child, for we are your children. You said, "Let the children come." Tonight we pray that as we have seen your promise fulfilled in Bethlehem so long ago, may we continue to prepare for you when you come again.
All: Amen.

Lesson For The Day: John 1:1-14

Pastor And Youth Advent Dialogue:
Advent Past, Present, And Future

Offering

Voluntary

Prayer:
Pastor: Heavenly Father, you have given to us your greatest gifts. Your promises to us have been fulfilled. May we respond in like measure to your steadfast love with the offering of our gifts — our treasures, our time, our talents. We join together in the prayer which you taught us. Our Father ...
All: Amen.
Pastor: Come, Lord Jesus,
All: Quickly come. Amen.

Closing Hymn:

Pastor And Youth Advent Dialogue

Advent Past, Present, And Future

(Bible verses in italics are not to be read aloud.)

Pastor: Welcome to our first Advent midweek service, (name).

Youth: Thanks, Pastor. I've been thinking about Advent and I have a lot of questions for you.

Pastor: What kind of questions?

Youth: Well, I looked up the word Advent in the dictionary, and it says a lot of different things. I wondered which one is the right definition.

Pastor: What did the dictionary say?

Youth: It says: "1) Arrival or coming into being, 2) the coming of Christ, and 3) the penitential period beginning four Sundays before Christmas." Which one is the church's definition of Advent? The last, I suppose?

Pastor: Actually they're all correct and are all part of our meaning of Advent. First, let's look at how the season of Advent originated, and how it leads us toward Epiphany.

Youth: I don't understand what you mean.

Pastor: The history of Christianity tells us that Epiphany was a special time for baptism. We know Epiphany celebrates the coming of the good news of Jesus to the Gentiles — the story of the Magi, but we also remember it as the time we celebrate Jesus' baptism by John the Baptizer. So it makes sense that Christians saw it as a time for *their* baptism. The Bible tells us to repent and be baptized. Therefore, Advent, like Epiphany, is a time for penitence, a time to think about our sins and ask for forgiveness as a preparation for baptism.

Youth: *Repentance* means to admit our sins and be sorry for them, then? Is that the same as penitence?

Pastor: Yes, but along with confessing your sins, you must try not to do those things again. You must improve and make amends — do something to show you're really sorry.

Youth: But I thought Lent is the time when we look at our sins. We feel bad and try to do better. We feel bad because Jesus died so that our sins would be forgiven. It sounds like Lent and Advent are the same.

Pastor: Well, it's similar, but a bit different. During *Lent*, we remember that Jesus died as a sacrifice on the cross because of our sins. We feel we caused Jesus' death. Because we feel Jesus' death is our fault, Lent is a time of sorrow, until Easter when Jesus rises from the dead. But *Advent* is a time of joy, not a time of sorrow. We feel joy because we are preparing to celebrate Jesus' birthday. Jesus is our Savior, born to destroy death and sin. So when Jesus is born, God's promise to care for us and give us eternal life is fulfilled. We are given a new birth in baptism. It is a little confusing.

Youth: It's like another chance. I think I understand. Let's say I did something wrong, and I was going to be punished. Then, my parents tell me that they forgive me, because they know I already suffered just knowing how bad I made them feel. They know I'm sorry and that I'll do better.

Pastor: Yes, something like that. It would be a time of joy then, not of sorrow.

Youth: But people get baptized all year long now, so Advent doesn't seem to fit that idea any more.

Pastor: Well, Advent has taken on some added dimensions over the years. As the other definitions in the dictionary say, we also think of Advent as a time of waiting and preparing.

Youth: Waiting, you mean for Christmas?

Pastor: Christmas is only one part of it. It is probably the one that comes to mind the quickest for most people — but there are two other types of preparation and waiting.

Youth: What do you mean?

Pastor: Our anticipation of Christmas looks toward our past. We think of Isaiah's words, "A shoot shall come out from the stump of Jesse, and a branch shall grow out of his roots" (*Isaiah 11:1*). And he continues, saying, "For a child has been born for us, a son given to us" (*Isaiah 9:6*). You see, Jesus was coming — his birth was prophesied. But the coming of Jesus is multi-layered, so our preparation gets complicated.

Youth: I think I understand the words from Isaiah, but what do you mean by multi-layered? I don't know what that means.

Pastor: Well, you understand Jesus came to us in the past — meaning his birth. But what do you think would be next? He came in the past and then what?

Youth: Well, I don't know for sure. In English class, we learn there's past, present, and future tenses.

Pastor: Great! You are correct. Besides the fact that Christ came in the past, which is Christmas, we also look for his coming in the present and the future.

Youth: I guess you are going to have to give me some help on this part.

Pastor: Let's look at the present. Isaiah said, "The people who walked in darkness have seen a great light; those who lived in a land of deep darkness — on them light has shined" (*Isaiah 9:2*). Let me explain it with an example. Can you think of a time when you were totally in the dark?

Youth: Sure, more than once. One night in a storm our lights went out at home, and we all bumped into everything and each other looking for candles and matches. But, most of all, I remember once when I was in a fun house at the fair. It was not only pitch-dark, it was scary — things grabbed at me. I could feel creepy things touching my skin. I didn't know which way to go or anything!

Pastor: That's a good example — because without Jesus, that's what life would be like — scary, hopeless, the Devil and his angels surrounding us. Pretty frightening! But Jesus brought the light, because he was the light. The apostle John tells us that Jesus said, "Walk while you have the light, so that the darkness may not overtake you. If you walk in the darkness, you do not know where you are going. While you have the light, believe in the light, so that you may become children of light" (*John 12:35-36*). As children of the light, meaning knowing Jesus and having him in our lives, we have a responsibility to the present — to today. We must keep the light shining. We must help others to know about Jesus. Jesus said, "No one after lighting a lamp puts it under the bushel basket, but on the lampstand, and it gives light to all the house. In the same way, let your light shine before others, so that they may see your good works and give glory to your Father in heaven" (*Matthew 5:15-16*). So you see, we should sing our carols of joy and spread the Good News, like the shepherds, all the year through.

Youth: In other words, as we get ready for Christmas, we should get ourselves ready for a full year of making Jesus' light shine.

Pastor: Yes, and we do this through his Word, through worshiping, praying, studying, and witnessing. We open our hearts and let his Word take seed and grow. And, finally, when we do that, we prepare for his future coming.

Youth: You mean like going to heaven?

Pastor: Yes, we're preparing for that, but also for the day when Jesus returns to earth, when he comes on earth to take believers with him to heaven. James writes, "Be patient, therefore, beloved, until the coming of the Lord. The farmer waits for the precious crop from the earth, being patient with it until it receives the early and the late rains. You also must be patient. Strengthen your hearts, for the coming of the Lord is near" (*James 5:7-8*). Jesus tells us he will come again and take us from the earth to heaven with him.

Youth: The word *Advent* sure has a lot of meanings.

Pastor: It does, and, in the next three weeks, we will learn more about the waiting, preparation, and penitence which Advent is all about. I'm glad you could be with me tonight. Thank you.

Youth: Thank you for helping me to a better understanding of Advent.

Worship Bulletin

Through The Eyes Of A Child

Advent II

Opening Statement: Psalm 24:7-10

Pastor: Lift up your heads, O gates! and be lifted up, O ancient doors! that the King of glory may come in.

All: Who is the King of glory? The Lord, strong and mighty, the Lord, mighty in battle.

Pastor: Lift up your heads, O gates! and be lifted up, O ancient doors! that the King of glory may come in.

All: Who is this King of glory? The Lord of hosts, he is the King of glory.

Opening Hymn:

Advent Responsory: Psalm 63:1-8

Pastor: O God, you are my God, I seek you, my soul thirsts for you; my flesh faints for you, as in a dry and weary land where there is no water. So I have looked upon you in the sanctuary, beholding your power and glory. Because your steadfast love is better than life, my lips will praise you. So I will bless you as long as I live; I will lift up my hands and call on your name.

All sing: "Come, Thou Long-Expected Jesus"   Traditional Tune
**Come, thou long-expected Jesus,
Born to set thy people free;
From our fears and sins release us;
Let us find our rest in thee.
Israel's strength and consolation,
Hope of all the earth thou art,
Dear desire of every nation,
Joy of every longing heart.**

Pastor: My soul is satisfied as with a rich feast, and my mouth praises you with joyful lips when I think of you on my bed, and meditate on you in the watches of the night; for you have been my help, and in the shadow of your wings I sing for joy. My soul clings to you; your right hand upholds me.

All sing: "Come, Thou Long-Expected Jesus" Traditional Tune
Born thy people to deliver,
Born a child, and yet a king;
Born to reign in us forever,
Now thy gracious kingdom bring.
By thine own eternal Spirit
Rule in all our hearts alone;
By thine all-sufficient merit
Raise us to thy glorious throne.

Preparation And Prayer: (1 John 3:1-3)
Pastor: See what love the Father has given us, that we should be called children of God; and that is what we are. The reason the world does not know us is that it did not know him. Beloved, we are God's children now; what we will be has not yet been revealed. What we do know is this: when he is revealed, we will be like him, for we will see him as he is. And all who have this hope in him purify themselves, just as he is pure.
Let Us Pray: Heavenly Father, we come to you with the joy and innocence of a child, for we are your children. You said, "Let the children come." Tonight we pray that as we have seen your promise fulfilled in Bethlehem so long ago, may we continue to prepare for you when you come again.
All: Amen.

Lesson For The Day: Isaiah 40:1-5

Pastor And Youth Advent Dialogue:
Jesus Came To Earth

Offering

Voluntary

Prayer:
Pastor: Heavenly Father, you have given to us your greatest gifts. Your promises to us have been fulfilled. May we respond in like measure to your steadfast love with the offering of our gifts — our treasures, our time, and our talents. We join together in the prayer which you taught us. Our Father who art in heaven ...
All: **Amen.**
Pastor: Come, Lord Jesus,
All: **Quickly come. Amen.**

Closing Hymn:

Pastor And Youth Advent Dialogue

Jesus Came To Earth

(Bible verses in italics are not to be read aloud.)

Pastor: Welcome to the second Advent midweek service, (name).

Youth: Hi, Pastor.

Pastor: Tonight we are going to talk about Advent as a time of reflection and preparation, a time of joyful penitence, because we know that God fulfilled his plan of salvation for us. Without God's salvation we would have been lost and condemned sinners.

Youth: Wow! That's a lot. Advent's also a busy time getting things ready for Christmas.

Pastor: Yes, it is. "Getting ready" are important words. Tonight, we will learn how John the Baptist helped to get the world ready for Jesus' coming, and we're going to see that as we wait for things to happen, just like Jesus' coming, it takes patience and preparation.

Youth: I don't think I'm very patient.

Pastor: Most of us aren't, and that's why, I suppose, the Old Testament prophets and the Gospel writers are constantly reminding us that we must be patient for Christ's coming.

Youth: Pastor, what is a *prophet*?

Pastor: A prophet is a person inspired by God to announce God's plan for our salvation. Hundreds of years before Jesus was on earth, God spoke through the prophets to tell the people that the Son of God would come to earth to win over death and the devil. A prophet even told about God's messenger who would come ahead of Jesus, before he began his ministry on earth, and who would announce Jesus' coming to all the people and prepare the way.

Youth: Was the messenger an angel?

Pastor: Often messengers are angels. In fact, an angel did appear to Joseph and Mary to prepare them for Jesus' birth, but God's messenger to all the people was John the Baptist, and through him, we learned much about being prepared. John, the son of Elizabeth and Zechariah, was a cousin of Jesus. This is what Isaiah said about John: "How beautiful upon the mountains are the feet of the messenger who announces peace, who brings good news, who announces salvation" (*Isaiah 52:7*). You see, in that passage, Isaiah referred to John as a messenger. And Isaiah called John a voice crying in the wilderness. This is what he said: "Prepare the way of the Lord, make straight in the desert a highway for our God. Every valley shall be lifted up, and every mountain and hill be made low; the uneven ground shall become level, and the rough places a plain. The glory of the Lord shall be revealed, and all people shall see it together, for the mouth of the Lord has spoken ... He shall feed his flock like a shepherd; he will gather the lambs in his arms, and carry them in his bosom, and gently lead the mother sheep" (*Isaiah 40:3-5, 11*).

Youth: The prophet sure knew a lot of stuff, and prophets said these things long before Jesus was born, didn't they?

Pastor: Yes, remember, the prophets were speaking words given to them by God. The apostle John, who was one of Jesus' disciples, talks about John the Baptist in this way: "There was a man sent from God, whose name was John. He came as a witness to testify to the light, so that all might believe through him. He himself was not the light, but he came to testify to the light. The true light, which enlightens everyone, was coming into the world" (*John 1:6-9*). Jesus was the light coming to a darkened world — meaning a hopeless, sinful world.

Youth: A lot of Bible verses call Jesus "the light." That means that Jesus helps us to see things clearly, just like a lamp or a light helps us to see where we're going.

Pastor: That's excellent; you do understand that very well. The apostle John wanted us to understand how important Jesus is to us. Listen to this verse again and tell me what you think Isaiah meant when he said, "He shall feed his flock like a shepherd; he will gather the lambs in his arms, and carry them in his bosom, and gently lead the mother sheep."

Youth: Sometimes, Jesus is called the "Good Shepherd," so he must be talking about Jesus. It sounds like he's telling us that Jesus will take care of us and guide us.

Pastor: That's correct. There are many analogies in the Bible. Analogies mean ways in which Jesus is described.

Youth: I know you just said that Jesus is also called *the light* in the Bible — and the light guides us, too!

Pastor: That's excellent. You're really listening. Let me read to you from another of Isaiah's prophecies. You'll hear another analogy about Jesus.

Youth: You mean *another* way Jesus is described?

Pastor: Correct. "A shoot shall come out from the stump of Jesse, and a branch shall grow out of his roots. The spirit of the Lord shall rest on him, the spirit of wisdom and understanding, the spirit of counsel and might, the spirit of knowledge and the fear of the Lord" (*Isaiah 11:1-2*). The prophet Jeremiah said almost the same thing: "The days are surely coming, says the Lord, when I will fulfill the promise I made to the house of Judah. In those days and at that time I will cause a righteous Branch to spring up for David; and he shall execute justice and righteousness in the land" (*Jeremiah 33:14-15*).

Youth: Sure, I see, Jesus is described as something growing — like a shoot or a branch. But you know what really is strange? It's how the prophets tell what family Jesus will be from and even in which city he will be born and everything.

Pastor: You have to remember that it is *God* talking through the prophets. Listen how the prophet Micah sums it all up: "But you, O Bethlehem of Ephrathah, who are one of the little clans of Judah, from you shall come forth for me one who is to rule in Israel, whose origin is from of old, from ancient days. Therefore he shall give them up until the time when she who is in labor has brought forth; then the rest of his kindred shall return to the people of Israel. And he shall stand and feed his flock in the strength of the Lord, in the majesty of the name of the Lord his God. And they shall live secure, for now he shall be great to the ends of the earth; and he shall be the one of peace" (*Micah 5:2-5*).

Youth: It seems like all the prophets are saying nearly the same thing, only a little bit differently. Micah calls Jesus a shepherd again, feeding his flock, and he mentions Bethlehem and that Jesus was the one of peace. It's like what the angels said when Jesus was born. It all fits together.

Pastor: That's true. You see, the prophets and John the Baptist were trying to prepare the people for the coming of the Son of God — the Messiah who would be the people's salvation. But I suppose you wonder what all of this has to do with patience. Remember, I said that's what we would talk about tonight. Let's hear what Jesus says about patience: "The kingdom of God is as if someone would scatter seed on the ground, and would sleep and rise night and day, and the seed would sprout and grow, he does not know how. The earth produces of itself, first the stalk, then the head, then the full grain in the head. But when the grain is ripe, at once he goes in with his sickle, because the harvest has come" (*Mark 4:26-29*).

Youth: Pastor, I think I understand. Once in a science project at school we were experimenting with seeds and how they grow. Each of us did something a little different — different kinds of soil, different fertilizer, different amounts of water and light. Then we had to wait.

Pastor: Gardening does take patience, doesn't it?

Youth: It seemed like everyone's seeds started growing except mine. I was really losing patience then. But finally mine started to grow — and it grew tall and strong. So I did learn that waiting takes patience — but it's worth it.

Pastor: It certainly is. So you understand how God planted the seed of his promise and it grew through the messages of the prophets and John the Baptist. As we look back to the days before Jesus was born and before his ministry began, we can understand how hard it was for the people to wait for God's promise. It takes much trust and faith.

Youth: We have it easy, though, because we know that Jesus was born, and the only thing we have to be patient for now is waiting for the celebration of his birth — Christmas. Sometimes I get impatient waiting for that.

Pastor: Christmas is certainly an exciting time. It has so many traditions and special treats, beautiful decorations reminding us of Jesus, and wonderful carols which have been sung for centuries. Even adults have a difficult time waiting. But in the next two weeks, we will be talking about *another* kind of waiting and preparation. Tonight, we've looked only at the *past*, and we have learned how God's wonderful plan, told us by the prophets, has been fulfilled already.

Youth: And we heard about all the ways that Jesus is described too, like a light, a shepherd, and a branch from the root of Jesse.

Pastor: Yes, descriptions help us see different qualities of Jesus, human born. Jesus holds us in his loving arms and guides us and offers us the light of his truth and the assurance of our salvation. But next we will learn what we should do in the *present* as we continue to wait and prepare for the future when Jesus will *return* to earth.

Youth: I wonder if I'll be here when he comes again.

Pastor: That's a question that has been asked by many people. In the next two weeks, we'll see what the Bible tells us about that. Thank you for being here.

Youth: Thank you for answering so many questions.

Worship Bulletin

Through The Eyes Of A Child
Advent III

Opening Statement: Psalm 24:7-10
Pastor: Lift up your heads, O gates! and be lifted up, O ancient doors! that the King of glory may come in.
All: **Who is the King of glory? The Lord, strong and mighty, the Lord, mighty in battle.**
Pastor: Lift up your heads, O gates! and be lifted up, O ancient doors! that the King of glory may come in.
All: **Who is this King of glory? The Lord of hosts, he is the King of glory.**

Opening Hymn:

Advent Responsory: Psalm 90:1-6, 12-17
Pastor: Lord, you have been our dwelling place in all generations. Before the mountains were brought forth, or ever you had formed the earth and the world, from everlasting to everlasting you are God. You turn us back to dust, and say, "Turn back, you mortals." For a thousand years in your sight are like yesterday when it is past, or like a watch in the night. You sweep them away; they are like a dream, like grass that is renewed in the morning; in the morning it flourishes and is renewed; in the evening it fades and withers.

All sing: "Come, Thou Long-Expected Jesus"   Traditional Tune
**Come, thou long-expected Jesus,
Born to set thy people free;
From our fears and sins release us;
Let us find our rest in thee.**

> **Israel's strength and consolation,**
> **Hope of all the earth thou art,**
> **Dear desire of every nation,**
> **Joy of every longing heart.**

Pastor: So teach us to count our days that we may gain a wise heart. Turn, O Lord! How long? Have compassion on your servants! Satisfy us in the morning with your steadfast love, so that we may rejoice and be glad all our days. Make us glad as many days as you have afflicted us, and as many years as we have seen evil. Let your work be manifest to your servants, and your glorious power to their children. Let the favor of the Lord our God be upon us, and prosper for us the work of our hands — O prosper the work of our hands!

All Sing: "Come, Thou Long-Expected Jesus"   Traditional Tune
> **Born thy people to deliver,**
> **Born a child, and yet a king;**
> **Born to reign in us forever,**
> **Now thy gracious kingdom bring.**
> **By thine own eternal Spirit**
> **Rule in all our hearts alone;**
> **By thine all-sufficient merit**
> **Raise us to thy glorious throne.**

Preparation And Prayer: (1 John 3:1-3)
Pastor: See what love the Father has given us, that we should be called children of God; and that is what we are. The reason the world does not know us is that it did not know him. Beloved, we are God's children now; what we will be has not yet been revealed. What we do know is this: when he is revealed, we will be like him, for we will see him as he is. And all who have this hope in him purify themselves, just as he is pure.
Let Us Pray: Heavenly Father, we come to you with the joy and innocence of a child, for we are your children. You

said, "Let the children come." Tonight we pray that as we have seen your promise fulfilled in Bethlehem so long ago, may we continue to prepare for you when you come again.
All: Amen.

Lesson For The Day: Matthew 24:37-44

Pastor And Youth Advent Dialogue:
Jesus Will Come Again

Offering

Voluntary

Prayer:
Pastor: Heavenly Father, you have given to us your greatest gifts. Your promises to us have been fulfilled. May we respond in like measure to your steadfast love with the offering of our gifts — our treasures, our time, our talents. We join together in the prayer which you taught us. Our Father ...
All: Amen.
Pastor: Come Lord Jesus,
All: Quickly come. Amen.

Closing Hymn:

Pastor And Youth Advent Dialogue

Jesus Will Come Again

(Bible verses listed in italics are not to be read aloud.)

Pastor: Tonight is our third Advent midweek service. Last week we learned about Isaiah and other prophets who told the people, long before Jesus was born, about God's plan for our salvation.

Youth: The prophet even knew about John the Baptist and about Bethlehem and all kinds of things.

Pastor: Yes. Because the prophets were inspired by God, they knew many things that would happen, and so they prepared the people for Jesus' coming.

Youth: The prophets prepared the people for the baby Jesus to be born in Bethlehem — but the Bible tells us that Jesus will come again. I'm not sure I understand that.

Pastor: We are told in many ways that there will be a second coming of Christ, and we will hear from the scriptures this evening and see if things become clearer for you.

Youth: But we won't all be alive when Jesus comes again, right?

Pastor: Correct, but no matter what, those who believe in him will be with him in heaven. This is part of God's plan.

Youth: So, we just have to wait and wonder?

Pastor: Listen to what James says: "Be patient, therefore, beloved, until the coming of the Lord. The farmer waits for the precious crop from the earth, being patient with it until it receives the early and the late rains. You also must be patient. Strengthen your hearts, for the coming of the Lord is near. Beloved, do not grumble against one another, so that you may not be judged. See, the Judge is standing at the doors! As an example of suffering and patience, beloved, take the prophets who spoke in the name of the Lord. Indeed, we call blessed those who showed endurance" (*James 5:7-11a*).

Youth: It sounds like James thought Jesus was coming right away. He says that "the coming of the Lord is near" and "the Judge is standing at the doors." What does that all mean?

Pastor: I think James is telling us that Jesus could come at any time. As humans, we do not understand God's time. We must be prepared for his coming — and we must be patient.

Youth: But what does he mean by "the Judge is standing at the door"?

Pastor: We know that Jesus' final coming will be the end of this world as we know it. It will be a time of judgment when believers will be separated from non-believers. Paul writes that on that last day, Jesus will come down from heaven on a cloud with the angels and that the unbelievers will be punished by sending them to destruction, separated from the presence of God for all eternity. Then the earth will be destroyed, and this world that we know will be gone.

Youth: That sounds frightening.

Pastor: You do not have to fear. Since you are a believer that would be a wonderful day. Paul says to those who are believers that this is how it will be on the last day: "For the Lord himself, with a cry of command, with the archangel's call and with the sound of God's trumpet, will descend from heaven, and the dead in Christ will rise first. Then we who are alive, who are left, will be caught up in the clouds together with them to meet the Lord in the air; and so we will be with the Lord forever" (*1 Thessalonians 4:16-17*).

Youth: I wonder when this will happen.

Pastor: The Bible says that Jesus will come like a thief in the night. In other words, his coming will be very unexpected, and so we don't have any idea when the end will be. Lots of people keep leading lives not pleasing to God and not listening to God's words, but one day there will be no more time. They will not have time to repent or to be sorry for their wrongdoing.

Youth: I sure know what you mean by that! Once when my parents went out, they told me that I should have all my homework done before they got back. Well, I thought I had lots of time, and so I stayed outside, and when I came in, my favorite television show was on. I figured I could hurry up and do my homework after the program. I sure got in trouble. My parents got home sooner than I expected, and I hadn't done one homework assignment.

Pastor: I bet they weren't very happy.

Youth: No, they weren't. I promised I wouldn't do that again. And I haven't. But I had time to say I was sorry. You said people who don't listen to God won't get that chance.

Pastor: You are very correct. The Bible tells that we can't wait for the last minute to prepare. We don't know when that minute will be. Mark says it this way: "But about that day or hour no one knows, neither the angels in heaven, nor the Son, but only the Father. Beware, keep alert; for you do not know when the time will come. It is like a man going on a journey, when he leaves home and puts his slaves in charge, each with his work, and commands the doorkeeper to be on the watch. Therefore, keep awake — for you do not know when the master of the house will come, in the evening, or at midnight, or at cockcrow, or at dawn, or else he may find you asleep when he comes suddenly" (*Mark 13:32-36*). That story sounds like your story, doesn't it?

Youth: Yes, it does. The sleeping people are probably the people who don't listen to God, right?

Pastor: Right.

Youth: So, Pastor, what can we do? As Christmas gets closer, all of us see people who are getting ready for the holiday. They are buying gifts and decorating and doing things, but they don't all come to church. They forget that Christmas celebrates Jesus' birth. How do we help them learn more about the real meaning of Christmas?

Pastor: That's a good question. The Bible tells us as Christians we have many things to do, because we are also God's disciples in the present day. Jesus said, "All authority in heaven and on earth has been given to me. Go therefore and make disciples of all nations, baptizing them in the name of the Father and of the Son and of the Holy Spirit, and teaching them to obey everything that I have commanded you. And remember, I am with you always, to the end of the age" (*Matthew 28:18-20*). Do you understand?

Youth: Yes. It means that because we believe, we should be helping others to know about Jesus and to be baptized.

Pastor: Yes, that is called the "great commission." Jesus has asked us to be witnesses to him in our daily lives. Sometimes it's difficult to do that, but it is what God expects.

Youth: That sounds like everyone has to be a missionary, though — or a pastor.

Pastor: Not at all. We must try to be like Christ in our lives. Jesus told the disciples, "I give you a new commandment: love one another; you must love one another just as I have loved you. It is by your love for one another that everyone will recognize you as my disciples" (*John 13:34-35*). Does that sound like something you can do?

Youth: You mean we are suppose to show kindness to people and be good? What about people who are not nice to us? It's hard to be kind back.

Pastor: Yes, it is not easy.

Youth: One day at school, one of the guys who's always pushing everyone around threw my books and papers in the wastebasket when I wasn't looking. If my friend hadn't noticed, I would have been in trouble.

Pastor: The Bible tells us if people cause us pain or hurt us in some way, we are to forgive them and try to help them. It is in this way we show our love. Think of Jesus on the cross when he prayed, "Father, forgive them."

Youth: I wanted to do something mean to that kid, not be nice to him. I wish I could be more like Jesus.

Pastor: All we can do is try. Each day we must pray and ask God to help us be more Christlike. That doesn't mean you can't have fun or that we have to live differently. You just have to think a little differently. Like, what did you do about the boy who threw your books away?

Youth: Nothing, I just got the books out of the wastebasket and didn't say anything.

Pastor: You did what was right. You didn't start a fight or cause trouble. Not everyone would have acted as you did. You see, you did what was right naturally. Now, let's continue. You mentioned how some people seem to leave Christ out of their celebration of Christmas. But I know that you and your family look forward to Christmas, not just because of the traditions and surprises associated with it. I know this because you worship regularly and you are joyful in your weekly celebration of your salvation. If each of us keeps that wonderful joy of Christmas in our hearts every day, we can serve as an example to others. As people wonder what makes Christians kind and loving, generous and full of peace, they will become more aware of Jesus. Imagine if the whole world were more loving and generous and peace-filled.

Youth: So that's what we can do, serve as examples for others?

Pastor: Yes. In our next midweek service, we will learn more about being a good example for others. Until then, remember Jesus' words, "It is by your love for one another that everyone will recognize you as my disciples" (*John 13:35*). Let's think about that during the week, (name).

Youth: I will, Pastor. Thanks.

Worship Bulletin

Through The Eyes Of A Child

Advent IV

Opening Statement: Psalm 24:7-10
Pastor: Lift up your heads, O gates! and be lifted up, O ancient doors! that the King of glory may come in.
All: **Who is the King of glory? The Lord, strong and mighty, the Lord, mighty in battle.**
Pastor: Lift up your heads, O gates! and be lifted up, O ancient doors! that the King of glory may come in.
All: **Who is this King of glory? The Lord of hosts, he is the King of glory.**

Opening Hymn:

Advent Responsory: Psalm 141:1-5, 8-10
Pastor: I call upon you, O Lord; come quickly to me; give ear to my voice when I call to you. Let my prayer be counted as incense before you, and the lifting up of my hands as an evening sacrifice. Set a guard over my mouth, O Lord; keep watch over the door of my lips. Do not turn my heart to any evil, to busy myself with wicked deeds in company with those who work iniquity; do not let me eat of their delicacies. Let the righteous strike me; let the faithful correct me. Never let the oil of the wicked anoint my head, for my prayer is continually against their wicked deeds.

All sing: "Come, Thou Long-Expected Jesus"   Traditional Tune
Come, thou long-expected Jesus,
Born to set thy people free;
From our fears and sins release us;
Let us find our rest in thee.

Israel's strength and consolation,
Hope of all the earth thou art,
Dear desire of every nation,
Joy of every longing heart.

Pastor: But my eyes are turned toward you, O God, my Lord; in you I seek refuge; do not leave me defenseless. Keep me from the trap that they have laid for me, and from the snares of evildoers. Let the wicked fall into their own nets, while I alone escape.

All sing: "Come, Thou Long-Expected Jesus"   Traditional Tune
Born thy people to deliver,
Born a child, and yet a king;
Born to reign in us forever,
Now thy gracious kingdom bring.
By thine own eternal Spirit
Rule in all our hearts alone;
By thine all-sufficient merit
Raise us to thy glorious throne.

Preparation And Prayer: (1 John 3:1-3)
Pastor: See what love the Father has given us, that we should be called children of God; and that is what we are. The reason the world does not know us is that it did not know him. Beloved, we are God's children now; what we will be has not yet been revealed. What we do know is this: when he is revealed, we will be like him, for we will see him as he is. And all who have this hope in him purify themselves, just as he is pure.
Let Us Pray: Heavenly Father, we come to you with the joy and innocence of a child, for we are your children. You said, "Let the children come." Tonight we pray that as we have seen your promise fulfilled in Bethlehem so long ago, may we continue to prepare for you when you come again.

All: **Amen.**

Lesson For The Day: Micah 5:2-5a

Pastor And Youth Advent Dialogue:
  Lord Jesus, Quickly Come

Offering

Voluntary

Prayer:
Pastor: Heavenly Father, you have given to us your greatest gift. Your promises to us have been fulfilled. May we respond in like measure to your steadfast love with the offering of our gifts — our treasures, our time, our talents. We join together in the prayer which you taught us. Our Father, who art in heaven ...
All: Amen.
Pastor: "Surely, I am coming soon," says the Lord.
All: Come, Lord Jesus. Amen.

Closing Hymn:

Pastor And Youth Advent Dialogue

Lord Jesus, Quickly Come

(Bible verses listed in italics are not to be read aloud.)

Pastor: Good evening. Here we are for our last Advent midweek service. Christmas is just around the corner.

Youth: It seems like it takes a long time waiting for Christmas, but we have been preparing for it for many weeks. I guess you're right when you said Advent is a time of patience and preparation.

Pastor: You just said some key words for Advent, didn't you? Patience. Preparation. We just need to add penitence and that sums it up. Tonight, we're going to focus on our penitence.

Youth: What does that mean — penitence?

Pastor: Penitence means to repent. It means we are sorry for the things we do which are wrong in God's sight and that we will do better. Daily we need to ask for forgiveness for our sins, and then work very hard to live a life which is God-pleasing.

Youth: It's very hard to be good all the time. Even when I mean to do the right thing, sometimes I don't. I do things I know are not good — like talking back to my parents or making up an excuse why my homework isn't done.

Pastor: If you know you have sinned and you are truly sorry, then you need to talk it over with God and make a real effort to improve. God has promised us forgiveness. As we receive forgiveness, we are excited to tell others, and as we tell others, we become disciples. We witness to others about God's plan for our salvation in our words and actions.

Youth: That's a big job, especially for someone who's not a pastor — someone young, like me.

Pastor: We can be witnesses in our daily lives in very simple and basic ways. Listen to the apostle Paul's beautiful words written to the Colossians and see how they give us guidelines for our lives. "As God's chosen ones, holy and beloved, clothe yourselves with compassion, kindness, humility, meekness, and patience. Bear with one another, and if anyone has a complaint against another, forgive each other; just as the Lord has forgiven you, so you must forgive. Above all, clothe yourselves with love, which binds everything together in perfect harmony. And let the peace of Christ rule in your hearts, to which indeed you were called in the one body. And be thankful. Let the word of Christ dwell in you richly; teach and admonish one another in all wisdom; and with gratitude in your hearts sing psalms, hymns, and spiritual songs to God. And whatever you do, in word or deed, do everything in the name of the Lord Jesus, giving thanks to God the Father through him" (*Colossians 3:12-17*).

Youth: That sounds like a big job. How can we do all those things?

Pastor: I imagine you already do many of the things Paul suggests. First of all, let's look at our behavior. What qualities did Paul list?

Youth: Well, I heard patience again — and kindness. Meekness, too — but isn't that like someone who's a coward — someone who people push around?

Pastor: Maybe a better word for meekness is *mild-mannered*. It means someone who is not angry — someone who considers others' opinions and who is patient with other people.

Youth: Oh — like not being *pushy* and wanting your own way.

Pastor: Yes. Paul also says we should have humility and compassion. Humility means *humble* — not bragging or conceited in our behavior. It means being willing to forgive.

Youth: Okay, I understand humble, but what's compassion?

Pastor: Compassion is being sensitive to other people's pain and sorrow, having sympathy for people with problems.

Youth: A boy in my school had his home burn down, and we took up a collection of food and clothing for the family and toys for the children. Is that what you mean?

Pastor: It certainly is. At Christmas, many people show compassion and kindness, don't they? They are concerned about the poor and needy, the homeless, the people who are elderly and who are ill. There are many groups taking up collections for people.

Youth: Here at church, we do that — and at my school, too.

Pastor: God would like us to show that kind of compassion and kindness all year long. There are many organizations that need money and goods which we can support. But even more immediate are people we know — here at church or in your school or in your neighborhood — who need your love and understanding.

Youth: Do people want us to help them, though? Some people may think we are making fun of them, or they don't trust us when we're nice; they're even afraid of us. I went to the house of a lady who lives on my corner to shovel her snow. She hardly opened the door, and she said that she didn't have money to pay me. I said that was okay; I'd do it anyway — but she acted frightened.

Pastor: Yes. I am sorry that our world has become frightening to some people. Not all people are kind and generous, and so people don't trust one another. This is why it is so important that Christians behave in the way God has commanded. If each of us were more kind and thoughtful, it would help to make the world a happier and safer place. In fact, here is what Luke said: "When you give a luncheon or a dinner, do not invite your friends or your brothers or your relatives or rich neighbors, in case they may invite you in return, and you would be repaid. But when you give a banquet, invite the poor, the crippled, the lame, and the blind. And you will be blessed, because they cannot repay you, for you will be repaid at the resurrection of the righteous" (*Luke 14:12-14*).

Youth: Oh, I understand. If the neighbor lady had paid me, it would have been like a job. Instead, when I finished shoveling her snow, she opened the door wide and looked at me in surprise, and said, "Thank you and God bless you."

Pastor: You see, she realized that you did something out of kindness. We, as Christians, are to work toward peace and harmony in the world. We are to encourage one another and teach one another the way God wants us to live. When you see someone treating a new student in your school badly, because of the color of that person's skin, nationality, or just because the student is new, you can be kind and encourage others to be kind. Adults can do the same in the workplace and in their neighborhoods.

Youth: I always think about how I would feel in a new school, and I try to be helpful and friendly.

Pastor: Good. The Bible says to treat your neighbor as you would like to be treated. We are to clothe ourselves in love, as Paul tells us. We know if we teach love and peace, as Jesus has commanded us, God will be with us always. This is God's promise.

Youth: We've learned a lot about God's promises the past few weeks, haven't we?

Pastor: Yes. The prophets and patriarchs knew of God's promise and saw it fulfilled in the birth of Jesus.

Youth: And God has promised that we will have a home in heaven when we die.

Pastor: Yes. As Christians, we have hope in our salvation, and we trust in God. When Mary was a very young woman, she learned that she was to be the mother of God's son. She could have approached God's plan with fear and anger; life was to be difficult for Mary. The responsibility to be the mother of God was great. But Mary's response serves as a wonderful example of hope and trust for all of us. Mary said, "My soul magnifies the Lord, and my spirit rejoices in God my Savior, for he has looked with favor on the lowliness of his servant. Surely, from now on all generations will call me blessed, for the Mighty One has done great things for me, and holy is his name" (*Luke 1:46-49*).

Youth: Listening to what Mary said, she doesn't seem to be afraid or anything. She just praises God!

Pastor: And as Christians, we, too, are to praise God. Paul said, "Rejoice in the Lord always; again I will say, rejoice. Let your gentleness be known to everyone. The Lord is near. Do not worry about anything, but in everything by prayer and supplication with thanksgiving let your requests be made known to God. And the peace of God, which surpasses all understanding, will guard your hearts and minds in Christ Jesus" (*Philippians 4:4-7*). You see, Mary had such trust in God that she did not question what he had planned for her to do; she just praised him for it. Now, we need to do the same.

Youth: I'm not sure what a kid can do. How can we know what God has planned for us?

Pastor: We know God has eternal life planned for those who believe in him, and since you are a believer, God has a place for you in heaven. But what can you do? Well, you've already mentioned a couple of things. You shoveled snow for the neighbor lady for no pay. You helped collect money and food for the boy from your school whose home was burned. That's what is meant. If you see a way you can show love or kindness to someone in need and you do it, it's what God asks. And remember, you also are God's witness, when you come to church and Sunday School.

Youth: Gosh, I do all of that!

Pastor: During this Advent season, we have taken a look at the plan that God prepared for us, how he gave us Jesus, born as a tiny baby in Bethlehem, who is our Savior. We have seen how he sent the message of salvation long before Jesus was born and prepared the way for his coming through the prophets and others, like John the Baptist. And we also know what God expects of us.

Youth: We're to be his disciples and have Christmas in our hearts all year long. And we should be generous and kind. And most of all, we are to show our love for others.

Pastor: You have learned a lot this Advent season. May our hearts be filled with the joy of that first Christmas, and may each of us follow Jesus' example in our love for one another. Thank you for being with me tonight, (name).

Youth: You're welcome, Pastor.

Worship Bulletin

Through The Eyes Of A Child

Christmas

Opening Statement: Isaiah 9:2, 6
Pastor: The people who walked in darkness have seen a great light; those who lived in a land of deep darkness — on them light has shined. For a child has been born for us, a son given to us; authority rests upon his shoulders; and he is named Wonderful Counselor, Mighty God, Everlasting Father, Prince of Peace.

Opening Hymn:

Christmas Responsory: Isaiah 11:1-3, 6
Pastor: A shoot shall come out from the stump of Jesse,
All: And a branch shall grow out of his roots.
Pastor: The spirit of the Lord shall rest on him,
All: The spirit of wisdom and understanding,
Pastor: The spirit of counsel and might,
All: The spirit of knowledge and the fear of the Lord.
Pastor: His delight shall be in the fear of the Lord.
All: He shall not judge by what his eyes see, or decide by what his ears hear;
Pastor: The wolf shall live with the lamb,
All: The leopard shall lie down with the kid,
Pastor: The calf and the lion and the fatling together,
All: And a little child shall lead them.

Preparation And Prayer: (1 John 3:1-3)
Pastor: See what love the Father has given us, that we should be called children of God; and that is what we are. The reason the world does not know us is that it did not know him.

Beloved, we are God's children now; what we will be has not yet been revealed. What we do know is this: when he is revealed, we will be like him, for we will see him as he is. And all who have this hope in him purify themselves, just as he is pure.

Let Us Pray: Heavenly Father, we come to you with the joy and innocence of a child, for we are your children. You said, "Let the children come." We come to you in prayer to thank you for this most precious gift, the birth of your Son, the Child born in Bethlehem so many years ago. May we continue to come to you in prayer and thanksgiving, until you come to us again, as you have promised.

All: **Amen.**

Hymn:

Gospel Reading: Luke 1:26-35

Pastor And Youth Dialogue:
Christmas Through The Eyes Of A Child

Part I — Dialogue

Hymn: "Of The Father's Love Begotten"   Traditional Tune
All: **Of the Father's love begotten**
Ere the worlds began to be,
He is Alpha and Omega,
He the source, the ending he,
Of the things that are, that have been,
And the future years shall see,
Evermore and evermore.

This is he whom seers in old time
Chanted of with one accord,
Whom the voices of the prophets
Promised in their faithful word;
Now he shines, the long-expected;

Let creation praise its Lord
Evermore and evermore.

Part II — Dialogue

Hymn: "O Little Town Of Bethlehem"   Traditional Tune
All: O little town of Bethlehem,
How still we see thee lie!
Above thy deep and dreamless sleep
The silent stars go by;
Yet in thy dark streets shineth
The everlasting light
The hopes and fears of all the years
Are met in thee tonight.

Part III — Dialogue

Hymn: "Away In A Manger"   Traditional Tune
All: Away in a manger, no crib for a bed,
The little Lord Jesus laid down his sweet head;
The stars in the sky looked down where he lay,
The little Lord Jesus asleep on the hay.

The cattle are lowing, the Baby awakes,
But little Lord Jesus, no crying he makes.
I love Thee, Lord Jesus; look down from the sky,
And stay by my cradle till morning is nigh.

Part IV — Dialogue

Hymn: "Angels We Have Heard On High"   Traditional Tune
All: Angels we have heard on high,
Sweetly singing o'er the plains,
And the mountains in reply,
Echoing their joyous strains.
(*Refrain*) Gloria in excelsis Deo.
Gloria in excelsis Deo.

Come to Bethlehem and see
Him whose birth the angels sing;
Come, adore on bended knee
Christ the Lord, the newborn king.
(*Refrain*) Gloria in excelsis Deo.
Gloria in excelsis Deo.

Part V — Dialogue

Hymn: "Hark! The Herald Angels Sing"   Traditional Tune

Offering

Voluntary

Service Of Lights:
Pastor: Jesus said, "I am the light of the world. Whoever follows me will never walk in darkness but will have the light of life." He is the true light coming from the Father, full of grace and truth. So let your light shine before others that they may see your good works and give glory to your Father in heaven.

(The ushers will come forward and light their candles from the pastor's candle. They will then give light to the first person in each row. That person will hold his candle toward the next person so each will light his candle. Tip only the unlighted candle. When everyone's candle is lit, the carol is sung.)

Hymn: "Silent Night"   Traditional Tune

Prayer: The Lord's Prayer

Pastor: Joy to the world, the Lord is come!
All: Glory to God in the highest!

Closing Hymn: "Joy To The World"   Traditional Tune

Pastor And Youth Christmas Dialogue

Christmas Through The Eyes Of A Child

(Bible verses listed in italics are not to be read aloud.)

Part I

Pastor: John the apostle writes, "See what love the Father has given us, that we should be called children of God, and that is what we are called" (*1 John 3:1*). Young and old, we are God's children. Tonight, (name), we will look at Christmas through the eyes of a child. It seems that Christmas brings out the child in us all. For weeks, we anticipated the joy of Christmas as we celebrate the most profound gift ever given — God's only son, born to redeem us from our sins and to offer us eternal life with God in heaven. For weeks families have prepared themselves and their homes for this occasion. As we look around us, we also see the beauty here in our church building — the tree, the garland, and special banners.

Youth: And the candles; that's what I like. It reminds me of what the prophet Isaiah said about Jesus, that he would be a light in the world of darkness.

Pastor: Yes. Isaiah said, "The people who walked in darkness have seen a great light; those who lived in a land of deep darkness — on them light has shined" (*Isaiah 9:2*). Prophets, hundreds of years before Jesus' birth, prepared the people for the coming of the Savior and Redeemer. God spoke through the prophets to the people, telling them about the plan for salvation that was formed from the very beginning.

Youth: Do you mean with Adam and Eve?

Pastor: Yes. In the Garden of Eden God said to them, "I will put enmity between you and the woman, and between your offspring and hers; he will strike your head, and you will strike his heel."

God was speaking of the Devil and saying how Jesus would conquer the Devil because salvation was ours through Jesus.

Youth: Did God know that Adam and Eve would sin and need salvation?

Pastor: When we were created in God's image, we were given the freedom to make choices, a free will. God knew that by giving us our own choices, we would need protection from our humanness.

Youth: Without the birth of Jesus, there would be no hope for us, would there? We should really be thankful and praise God.

Carol: "Of The Father's Love Begotten"   Traditional

Part II

Youth: Pastor, what did Joseph do when he learned that Mary was going to have a baby?

Pastor: After Joseph was engaged and he found out that Mary was expecting a baby, he was very upset and confused. Joseph was a kind man and did not want to hurt Mary or embarrass her — but he didn't think he should marry her. He thought he would dismiss her quietly.

Youth: But he did marry her, right?

Pastor: Yes. Before Joseph could do what he had planned, an angel appeared to him in a dream and explained that the child to be born was God's son, conceived by the Holy Spirit, and was to be the Savior of the people.

Youth: So then he understood and wasn't upset anymore?

Pastor: Joseph did understand and he did as the angel said. He took Mary as his wife and named the baby Jesus, which means God is with us.

Youth: You said Joseph was upset when he found out about Mary. I suppose Mary was upset too.

Pastor: An angel also visited Mary and helped her to understand.

Youth: Was Mary frightened? What did she do?

Pastor: Mary was frightened and very confused, because the angel said, "Greetings, favored one!" Mary didn't know what that meant. But the angel told her not to be afraid. Then, the angel explained that she had been chosen by God and that she would have a baby boy who would be named Jesus.

Youth: Did Mary understand all this when the angel explained it?

Pastor: Mary was confused, because she had no husband and didn't understand how she could have a baby. The angel explained that Jesus was conceived by the Holy Spirit — and was God's son.

Youth: Then Mary must have felt better. She understood why the angel said, "Greetings, favored one."

Pastor: Yes, she did, and instead of being worried about the responsibility she had been given, she praised the Lord in a wonderful statement which we call *The Magnificat*. It begins, "My soul magnifies the Lord and my spirit rejoices in God my Savior" (*Luke 1:47*). Mary humbly accepted God's plan for her.

Youth: Pastor, why did Mary and Joseph go to Bethlehem when the baby Jesus was so close to being born? Maybe they should have waited.

Pastor: Emperor Augustus decreed that all people must register for a tax. The registration had to be done in the city from which the family came. Since Joseph was a descendant of David, they had to go to Bethlehem for the registration. Also, you know the message of the prophets said that Jesus would come from the family of David and be born in Bethlehem. So this was done to fulfill the prophecy.

Youth: So God planned it that way all along.

Pastor: That's right. God's plan was laid before the earth was created.

Youth: But wasn't the trip to Bethlehem hard for Mary?

Pastor: Certainly it was a difficult trip. Roads were rough. As tradition tells us, Joseph used a burro or donkey to help transport Mary — but even then, it took days, and when they arrived in Bethlehem their problems had only just begun.

Carol: "O Little Town Of Bethlehem"   Traditional

Part III

Youth: When my family travels, we don't have problems getting a hotel. Why did Joseph and Mary have so much trouble getting a room?

Pastor: You must remember that many people had to travel to the home of their ancestors to register for the tax. Bethlehem was not a big city, and so there were not many inns or rooms available. Many, many people crowded into the town. I would imagine families even opened their homes to relatives who came to register.

Youth: Why did the innkeeper put Mary and Joseph in a stable? That didn't seem very nice.

Pastor: First, you need to understand something about the stable. In those days, the stable was usually connected to the house or inn. Animals were important to the people for food and transportation — so the stables were clean and filled with fresh straw. I suppose when the innkeeper realized that Mary was going to have the baby very soon, he thought it was important that they have someplace to rest and keep warm. The stable was probably the best thing he could offer.

Youth: Did the innkeeper know it was God's son being born?

Pastor: Well, I don't suppose so. If he had, he might have given up his own bed. What do you think?

Youth: I would have, for sure.

Carol: "Away In A Manger"   Traditional

Part IV

Pastor: So Jesus was born that night and placed in a manger.

Youth: Pastor, what actually is a manger?

Pastor: A manger is a food trough for the animals. It made a little crib for the baby Jesus to rest.

Youth: Why would God plan it that way? Jesus should have been born in a palace or someplace like that.

Pastor: Jesus came into the world to bring salvation to all people. He was a man of humility and gentleness. God probably wanted people to see him in that way, not as a powerful king. People needed to know Jesus was an ordinary man.

Youth: Then after he was born, is that why God had the angels tell the shepherds first — because they were plain, ordinary people too?

Pastor: Yes, that's probably right. Imagine the wonder of that night! Like any night for the shepherds, they were probably sitting around a fire talking or singing — maybe even singing psalms like ones written by David, who was also a shepherd.

Youth: Did they see the star, do you think?

Pastor: Well, they were familiar with the night sky. They watched it every evening, so I suppose they would notice something unusual — maybe a star or a strange glow perhaps.

Youth: And then the angel came. Were they afraid?

Pastor: You can imagine they would be. Suddenly the sky glowed with a strange heavenly light and an angel sent from God appeared and said, "Do not be afraid; for see — I am bringing you good news of great joy for all the people; to you is born this day in the city of David a Savior, who is the Messiah, the Lord" (*Luke 2:10-11*).

Youth: I bet they were shaking and excited, too.

Pastor: I'm sure they were. They had waited a long time for the promised Messiah. They probably grabbed at each other and covered their eyes. Maybe they even fell on their knees. But they listened to the angel, and then a host of angels appeared, all singing praises to God.

Youth: I know about that. *Glory to God in the highest and on earth peace*. That's what they said.

Carol: "Angels We Have Heard On High"   Traditional

Part V

Youth: After the angels left, how did the shepherds know where to go to find Jesus?

Pastor: Well, if you remember, they knew he was born in Bethlehem, and the angel said, "You will find a child wrapped in bands of cloth and lying in a manger" (*Luke 2:12*). Because of this, they would know he was in a stable or a barn.

Youth: I know, they could follow the light also.

Pastor: I would imagine. But we know they did find Mary and Joseph and the baby, and the Bible says they fell down and worshiped Jesus.

Youth: That would have been so exciting to be one of those shepherds! I bet they ran back to tell the others what happened.

Pastor: The Bible says they told everyone they met about the marvelous things they saw and heard. Mary and Joseph must have been awed also by what the shepherds told them about the angels and the message from God. You know, I believe that God would like us to be like the shepherds — telling everyone that we meet in our lives about the wonder of that night and about God's promise fulfilled for us — our Light in the darkness!

Youth: Right — our Savior.

Pastor: Let's join together in saying the words of the angels. (*Youth joins in*) "Glory to God in the highest heaven, and on earth peace among those whom he favors" (*Luke 2:14*).

Carol: "Hark! The Herald Angels Sing"　　　　　　　Traditional

Worship Bulletin

Through the Eyes of a Child

Epiphany

Opening Statement: Revelation 22:16-17; Ephesians 5:8
Pastor: It is I, Jesus, who sent my angel to you with this testimony for the churches. I am the root and the descendant of David, the bright morning star. The Spirit and the bride say, "Come." And let everyone who hears say, "Come." And let everyone who is thirsty come. Let anyone who wishes take the water of life as a gift. For once you were darkness, but now in the Lord you are light. Live as children of light.

Opening Hymn:

Epiphany Responsory: Isaiah 60:1-5, 6b
Pastor: Arise, shine; for your light has come,
All: And the glory of the Lord has risen upon you.
Pastor: For darkness shall cover the earth,
All: And thick darkness the peoples;
Pastor: But the Lord will arise upon you,
All: And his glory will appear over you.
Pastor: Nations shall come to your light,
All: And kings to the brightness of your dawn.
Pastor: Lift up your eyes and look around;
All: They all gather together, they come to you;
Pastor: Your sons shall come from far away,
All: And your daughters shall be carried on their nurses' arms.
Pastor: Then you shall see and be radiant;
All: Your heart shall thrill and rejoice,

Pastor: Because the abundance of the sea shall be brought to you,
All: **The wealth of the nations shall come to you.**
Pastor: They shall bring gold and frankincense,
All: **And shall proclaim the praise of the Lord.**

New Testament Reading: Ephesians 3:2-12

Preparation And Prayer: (1 John 3:1-3)
Pastor: See what love the Father has given us, that we should be called children of God; and that is what we are. The reason the world does not know us is that it did not know him. Beloved, we are God's children now; what we will be has not yet been revealed. What we do know is this: when he is revealed, we will be like him, for we will see him as he is. And all who have this hope in him purify themselves, just as he is pure.
Let Us Pray: Heavenly Father, we come to you with the joy and innocence of a child, for we are your children. You said, "Let the children come." We pray that as we have seen your promise fulfilled in Bethlehem so long ago, may we continue to prepare for you when you come again.
All: Amen.

Gospel Hymn: "As With Gladness Men Of Old" Traditional Tune
All: **As with gladness men of old**
Did the guiding star behold;
As with joy they hailed its light,
Leading onward, beaming bright;
So, most gracious Lord, may we
Evermore be led by thee.

As with joyful steps they sped,
Savior, to thy lowly bed,
There to bend the knee before
Thee, whom heav'n and earth adore;
So may we with willing feet
Ever seek thy mercy seat.

Gospel Reading: Matthew 2:1-12

Gospel Hymn: "As With Gladness Men Of Old" Traditional Tune
All: Holy Jesus, every day
Keep us in the narrow way;
And when earthly things are past,
Bring our ransomed souls at last
Where they need no star to guide,
Where no clouds thy glory hide.

In the heavenly country bright
Need they no created light;
Thou its light, its joy, its crown,
Thou its sun which goes not down;
There forever may we sing
Alleluias to our King.

Pastor And Youth Epiphany Dialogue:
Epiphany Through The Eyes Of A Child

Prayers Of The Day: *(Concluding with following)*
Pastor: Heavenly Father, we thank you for this gift of light, a light which has reached into our darkened world and filled it with hope and salvation.
All: **May our light shine in this world, so that we may serve as a reflection of your greater light. Amen.**
Pastor: The peace of the Lord, our Morning Star, be with you always.
All: **And also with you.**

Offering

Voluntary

The Eucharist: (from John 1:1-5, 12-14)
Pastor: In the beginning was the Word, and the Word was with God, and the Word was God.

All: He was in the beginning with God. All things came into being through him, and without him not one thing came into being.
Pastor: What has come into being in him was life, and the life was the light of all people.
All: The light shines in the darkness, and the darkness did not overcome it.
Pastor: But to all who received him, who believed in his name, he gave power to become children of God, who were born, not of blood or of the will of the flesh or of the will of man, but of God.
All: And the Word became flesh and lived among us, and we have seen his glory, the glory as of a father's only son, full of grace and truth.

The Words Of Institution

The Lord's Prayer

Distribution Of The Body And Blood Of Christ

Dismissal:
Pastor: May the body and blood of Jesus Christ, the Morning Star, give light to those who sit in darkness and guide our feet into the way of peace.
All: Amen.

Benediction:
Pastor: The Lord bless you and keep you, and make his light to shine upon you, and give you peace.
All: Amen.
Pastor: Go forth in joy. Let your lights shine!
All: Thanks be to God!

Closing Hymn:

Pastor And Youth Epiphany Dialogue

Epiphany Through The Eyes Of A Child

(Bible verses listed in italics are not to be read aloud.)

Pastor: "Arise, shine; for your light has come, and the glory of the Lord has risen upon you" *(Isaiah 60:1)*. Today, we celebrate Epiphany — when Christ is revealed to the world.

Youth: What does that mean, Pastor?

Pastor: Let's look at it this way. In Advent, we celebrated the coming of Christ. Christmas celebrated his arrival — his birth. Epiphany celebrates Christ's presence in our lives. Jesus was born in Bethlehem — his background is Jewish — but Epiphany celebrates the coming of Jesus to the Gentiles.

Youth: Are we Gentiles?

Pastor: We sure are. Gentiles are people who are not Jewish — which, in our situation, means people who are Christian.

Youth: How old was Jesus when he came to the Gentiles?

Pastor: Well, Jesus didn't actually come to the Gentiles in that sense. The Gentiles actually came to him — in the form of the Magi — the three Wise Men. Jesus was still a baby.

Youth: Who were the Wise Men? And why did they come to see Jesus?

Pastor: It was all part of God's plan that the whole world would have knowledge of Jesus, the Savior. God planned it from the very beginning. In fact, just as Jesus' birth was prophesied, so was the coming of Christ to the Gentiles prophesied. Isaiah said, "The root of Jesse shall come, the one who rises to rule the Gentiles; in him the Gentiles shall hope" (*Romans 15:12*). And Isaiah also wrote, "A multitude of camels shall cover you, the young camels of Midian and Ephah; all those from Sheba shall come. They shall bring gold and frankincense, and shall proclaim the praise of the Lord" (*Isaiah 60:6*).

Youth: He was talking about the Wise Men, right?

Pastor: Yes, that's right. Even the Wise Men were prophesied by the prophets. But, you asked who the Wise Men are. The Wise Men are known by many names: Magi, Kings, Stargazers, and even Priests. Actually, from what history tells us, the Wise Men were men who had learned about medicine, natural sciences, and astrology, which is the study of the positions of the stars and planets in the sky. They believed that these changes and movements of heavenly bodies affected things that happened on the earth.

Youth: So, because they knew about all of those things, people thought they were wise.

Pastor: Rulers would often want these Wise Men to help them make decisions — to foretell the future, in a way.

Youth: Isn't that wrong? We aren't suppose to believe in that, are we? It's like magic.

Pastor: If you think about it, *magi* is like another word for magician. I suppose the difference is that the Wise Men also studied religious teachings. Those who came from Persia believed very much like the Jews, and they were looking for the Messiah. They believed in one God and, in fact, believed that light was a symbol of God. So as they studied the sky and saw this strange light, a star that they did not recognize, they believed that it was a sign that the Messiah had come to earth.

Youth: Did they know who the Messiah was or why he came to earth?

Pastor: Many of the Magi knew the Messiah was promised by God and that he would come to save the people from their sins. They thought of him as a king, and so that explains why Herod was so frightened when he learned of this.

Youth: What do you mean? What did he do?

Pastor: As I mentioned, often the kings and emperors would have a staff of Wise Men who would help them make decisions and tell them about all the things they thought might happen in the future; Herod was among them. Herod, who was appointed king of Judea and who also took control of Jerusalem as well, was a very bloodthirsty and evil ruler. He was responsible for many terrible deaths, including members of his own family. When the Wise Men from the East came to Jerusalem, they asked, "Where is the child who has been born king of the Jews?" (*Matthew 2:2*). Herod moved quickly into action. He was frightened and gathered his chief priests and scribes around him and demanded to know where this child was to be born. They searched the sacred scriptures and found the writings of the prophet Micah, which named Bethlehem as the birthplace of Jesus.

Youth: So we know that Jesus would have trouble with Herod.

Pastor: Exactly. Herod summoned the Wise Men and told them to go to Bethlehem. He also ordered them to return when they had found the baby and let him know the exact location. He lied and said he wanted to go and honor the child, but we know he had other plans.

Youth: Was he planning to get rid of the king — to kill Jesus?

Pastor: Yes, because Herod saw Jesus as a threat to his power. He thought Jesus, King of the Jews, was an *earthly* king. The Wise Men did follow the star and found Jesus in a house in Bethlehem and they knelt before him and opened their treasure chests and gave him gifts of gold, frankincense, and myrrh.

Youth: So what happened when they told Herod where he was?

Pastor: That is a wonderful part of the story. In a dream they were warned not to return to Herod, and so they went to their homelands by a different way and never did return to Herod.

Youth: Herod must have been angry. But we know he didn't find Jesus, right?

Pastor: When Herod, who was very ill and nearing death, realized that the Wise Men were not returning as he had ordered, he was very angry. He ordered his soldiers to find all children two years old or less in and around Bethlehem and kill them. This was also prophesied by Jeremiah.

Youth: That was terrible. How did Jesus get saved?

Pastor: An angel appeared to Joseph in a dream, saying, "Get up, take the child and his mother, and flee to Egypt, and remain there until I tell you; for Herod is about to search for the child, to destroy him" (*Matthew 2:13*). So Joseph immediately, during the night, took Mary and Jesus out of Bethlehem to Egypt where they stayed until the death of Herod. This also was foretold by the prophet Hosea, who said, "Out of Egypt I have called my son" (*Hosea 11:1*).

Youth: Wow! Joseph and Mary had a very hard time keeping Jesus safe, didn't they? The Bible prophesied so many things that happened. So is that the whole story of Epiphany?

Pastor: We certainly talked about the incidents that involved Jesus and his family and the fulfillment of the prophecies, yes. But remember, Epiphany is also the time that the Gentiles learned about Jesus, remember?

Youth: How does all that fit in?

Pastor: Well, the Wise Men came from other countries than the lands of the Jews. So when the Wise Men came seeking the baby Jesus, they were the first Gentiles to acknowledge that Jesus was the long-awaited Messiah. These men had followed the star from, perhaps, Mesopotamia, Persia, Chaldea, or Media, lands east of Judea. We also know that as the Jews moved into these other countries, some as captives and some by choice, they also spread the hope and promise of a divine Redeemer to the people in those lands.

Youth: Does the Bible tell us any more about the Wise Men?

Pastor: No, the Bible gives us no more facts, but there are many traditions associated with the Wise Men. Some traditions say that the three Wise Men were Melchior, King of Arabia, who brought gold to Jesus; Gaspar, the King of Tarsus, who brought Jesus myrrh; and Balthasar, King of Ethiopia, who brought Jesus frankincense as a gift.

Youth: Those seem like strange gifts to give a baby, don't they? Why did they give them those gifts?

Pastor: All of the gifts are significant. Gold is certainly of value, so there is no need to explain why that was given. Myrrh is a very fragrant oil or resin which is taken from a tree and is used as a cosmetic, but most importantly as a medicine for healing and purification. It was even used in embalming. Frankincense is a resin which also comes from a tree, and it is used as an incense which is burned for religious purposes. It gives off a strong, steady flame and releases an odor, like incense, when burned.

Youth: But I still don't understand.

Pastor: Symbolically, we can see that these items represent the different aspects of Christ: precious gold for Christ the King, healing myrrh for Christ the Great Physician, and sacrificial frankincense for Christ the High Priest. Remember, this is not in the Bible; it is only tradition. The important part is that these men were Gentiles, and it was the beginning of the growth of Christianity. Epiphany explains how the news of Jesus, as our Savior, was spread all around the world.

Youth: I guess that is still part of our job, too — to spread the Word of God to people who don't go to church.

Pastor: Indeed, it is. Being a missionary — or one who spreads the message of salvation — is not easy today, no more than it was in biblical times. The apostle Paul tells us about his experiences as a missionary. "The next Sabbath almost the whole city gathered to hear the word of the Lord. But when the Jews saw the crowds, they were filled with jealousy; and blaspheming, they contradicted what was spoken by Paul. Then both Paul and Barnabas spoke out boldly, saying, 'It was necessary that the word of God should be spoken first to you. Since you reject it and judge yourselves to be unworthy of eternal life, we are now turning to the Gentiles. For so the Lord has commanded us saying, *I have set you to be a light for the Gentiles, so that you may bring salvation to the ends of the earth.*' When the Gentiles heard this, they were glad and praised the word of the Lord; and as many as had been destined for eternal life became believers. The word of the Lord spread throughout the region. But the Jews incited the devout women of high standing and the leading men of the city, and stirred up persecution against Paul and Barnabas, and drove them out of their region. So they shook the dust off their feet in protest against them, and went to Iconium. And the disciples were filled with joy and with the Holy Spirit" (*Acts 13:44-52*). Paul and others like him serve as an example for us. We see that despite discouragement and difficult times, they continued to spread God's Word and did it with joy and with the power of the Holy Spirit.

Youth: It takes a lot of courage to do that.

Pastor: Yes, our discipleship is not easy. Helping the community of believers to grow has been given to us as a commandment of Jesus, remember, to go into all the world teaching and baptizing in the name of the Father, Son, and Holy Spirit. So as we go into our daily lives spreading God's Word through our words and our actions, remember that Jesus gave us another commandment which will guide us. "I give you a new commandment: love one another; you must love one another just as I have loved you. It is by your love for one another that everyone will recognize you as my disciples" (*John 13:34-35*). It is this new commandment that guides our own Epiphany.

Youth: And sharing love is another way we let our light shine.

Pastor: It sure is. Let each of us be disciples and continue the work of Paul and Barnabas and all of the saints before us. Thank you for being with us tonight, (name).

Youth: Thank you, Pastor, and I will remember that it is by love that people will know me as a disciple of Jesus.

www.ingramcontent.com/pod-product-compliance
Lightning Source LLC
Chambersburg PA
CBHW071751040426
42446CB00012B/2518